(IS THIS THE WAY TO) AMARII

WORDS AND MUSIC BY NEIL SEDAKA AND HOWARD GREENFIELD

ISBN10: 0-571-52864-3
EAN13: 978-0-571-52864-6

FABER *ff* MUSIC

FABER MUSIC · 3 QUEEN SQUARE · LONDON
fabermusic.com

Printed in England by Caligraving Ltd

9 780571 528646 >